S0-BMS-322

FOR THOSE IN LOVE

# For Those in Love

*Making Your Marriage Last a Lifetime*

LIONEL A. WHISTON

Abingdon Press
Nashville

FOR THOSE IN LOVE

*Copyright © 1983 by Abingdon Press*

All rights reserved.
No part of this book may be reproduced in any manner whatsoever without written permission of the publisher except brief quotations embodied in critical articles or reviews. For information address Abingdon Press, Nashville, Tennessee.

**Library of Congress Cataloging in Publication Data**

WHISTON, LIONEL A.
For those in love.
1. Marriage—Religious aspects—Christianity.
I. Title.
BV835.W53 1983 248.4 82-11524

**ISBN 0-687-13285-1**

Scripture quotations unless otherwise noted are from the Revised Standard Version Common Bible, copyrighted © 1973 by the Division of Christian Education of the National Council of Churches of Christ in the U.S.A., and are used by permission.

The scripture quotation noted NEB is from the New English Bible. © the Delegates of the Oxford University Press and the Syndics of the Cambridge University Press 1961, 1970. Reprinted by permission.

The scripture quotation noted Moffatt is from The Bible: A New Translation, by James Moffatt; copyright 1935 by Harper & Row.

The poetry on page 44 is from the poem "Morning Has Broken" by Eleanor Farjeon. Reprinted by permission of Harold Ober Associates Incorporated. Copyright © 1957 by Eleanor Farjeon.

Illustrations and dust jacket cover design by Nancy G. Johnstone

MANUFACTURED BY THE PARTHENON PRESS AT
NASHVILLE, TENNESSEE, UNITED STATES OF AMERICA

*To those who read this book:*
*May you know the joy of the*
*ever-growing love that God*
*has in store for you.*

# CONTENTS

# FOREWORD

*For Those in Love* is a beautiful stroll with Lee and Irma Whiston through the heartaches and celebrations of marriage. The confessional story of their own marriage gives encouragement to those who are engaged and dreaming dreams of the future, those who are struggling to understand their spouse and keep a marriage intact, and those who want to keep growing in their celebrations of love. Lee unmasks our selfish, yet guilt-ridden, possessiveness of our own turf. Our calculated kindness to achieve results, withdrawal to punish, explosive anger to cover up hurt, our highlighting of faults rather than affirmation of gifts and efforts—those and many other failings need recognition and resolution. Lee Whiston gives us simple, common-sense recommendations for bringing a real and joyful love into our marriages.

You will laugh and cry with Irma and Lee. In the descriptions of pain, stubbornness, guilt, rejoicing, and serendipities, you will recognize your own emotions. Again and again you will say, "I know the

feeling"; "That's where I am"; and "That's where I want to be."

Each couple contemplating marriage will find advance notice of the pitfalls that lead to tension and the hope that can be fulfilled in a beautiful relationship. Those who are discovering growing separation and difficulty in their marriage will gain new insights into themselves and the emotions of their spouse. They will also receive steps to recapture the lost love. Those with happy marriages will perceive new and creative ways to greater fulfillment. This book will complement a pastor's counseling program.

There are practical suggestions for dealing with anger and differences as well as for building affirmation and praise. Real listening to the other is found in the ability to "move over into the center of another's being so that our insight and love spring up from where he or she is rather than from where we are."

Central to a celebration of love in marriage is the

presence of God. Both Lee and Irma have known the suffering of death and pain, and affirm hope for the future, for with God "you stand hand in hand, laughing together, weeping together." In each chapter the reader is helped to see the power and love of God bringing deeper understanding to one's own attitudes, of the emotions of the spouse, and of a growing, exciting relationship. The final chapter gives a brief and exciting explanation of the meaning of the marriage service itself.

In a day when marriages need hope and strength to build lasting commitments, *For Those in Love* is refreshing. The two of us read it aloud together. We recommend this process. We are grateful for the honesty, struggles, hurts, and joys that Lee and Irma share with the reader. What a model of sharing and caring!

*George and Carolyn Bashore*

George and Carolyn Bashore live and serve in the Boston area, where he is the resident bishop of The United Methodist Church.

# FOR THOSE IN LOVE

# INTRODUCTION

This book is written for those who believe in love. I wrote it at the urging of the Rev. Robert P. Stokes of State College, Pennsylvania. Bob said: "I have nothing to put in the hands of couples that I have counseled in preparation for marriage. I wanted something that is based on God and love, that grows out of experience, and that will be a guide through the perplexities and adventure of life together."

It springs out of countless pastoral and counseling experiences with couples and out of sixty-five years of married life. My wife and I have discussed together every chapter of this book, and I have not merely her permission but her enthusiastic approval in sharing the intimate experiences related here.

Needless to say, the book has a masculine bias. I have tried, however, to make it nonsexist, seeing each partner of the marriage as a child of God. At the same time, I have been true to my own experience.

As I have repeatedly implied, the closer Irma and I have been drawn together, the more real has been the presence of God. The corollary has also been

true: sincere closeness to God has resulted in a closer bond between Irma and me.

My prime thanks must be to Irma, without whose love and presence these experiences would not have occurred. She has stayed by me in sickness and health, whether richer or poorer. She has loved me through my introversion and withdrawals and has had unbounded faith in me. I can truly echo George Burns' words quoted at the beginning of chapter 3.

I am indebted to Bob Stokes for the initial idea of the book as well as for his wise counsel. I am indebted to my son, Dr. Lionel A. Whiston, Jr., of Eden Theological Seminary, who has made many valuable criticisms and suggestions. My thanks to Allen and Doris Clark, William and Nancy Udall, Roland and Julie Lane, Philip and Debbie Graham, and Dorothy Whiston, who read the manuscript and made helpful suggestions. Again I am indebted to my secretary, Phyllis Bailey, who has wrestled with my handwriting, patiently typing and retyping.

From someone in love to others in love—

*Lee Whiston*

Since my name and personal experiences in Lee's and my marriage are referred to in this book, it would be appropriate for me to include a comment. Little children so often say to parent or teacher, "Tell me a really truly story." And are we not—all of us—like children in this way? We enjoy true experiences rather than theoretical or fictional narratives. This book has told of the discoveries of sixty-five years of happy fellowship. There was a popular song in the thirties, mourning of lost love, "The thrill is gone!" Well, we have found the thrill need not be gone! Indeed each succeeding year proves to be "sweeter as the years go by"!

*Irma Mary Whiston*

CHAPTER ONE

# Opposites Attract

Why couldn't likes get married sometimes? Why always had opposites to pull each other? It must be some wise plan of the Lord to keep the pretty from getting prettier and the homely homelier, the sweet sweeter and the mean meaner. But if so, the devil had spiked the way of the Lord. Little did those opposites know a standing up before the preacher promising to love each other 'til death did them part, little did they know what they carried inside themselves against each other.

*—Conrad Richter*

Wouldn't it be convenient if people of similar temperaments always fell in love with each other? Then the money spenders would have a ball together, the schedule-minded pair would never be late for appointments, and in the orderly couple's house not a dish, magazine, or slipper would be out of place. But God does not make life that easy for us. It is persons of opposite temperaments who are most frequently drawn together.

The quiet one selects a talkative spouse. The happy-go-lucky skylark is drawn to the schedule-minded mate. One half of a pair will become a permissive parent and the other a nonpermissive disciplinarian. Often the frugal marry the extravagant. The always-on-time is yoked to the never-on-time. The cautious, deliberate one is tied to the carefree plunger. One partner will act before thinking; the other will think so long that he or she fails to act at all. Couples are often alike in ideals and goals, but their temperaments not merely differ but are often diametrically opposed to each other.

It is easy to see God's wisdom in this plan. If the happy-go-lucky always married the happy-go-lucky couldn't-care-less, and if the quiet introvert married a similar mate, their children would be doubly predisposed in those directions and their children in turn would be quadruply so. Thus the race would go out of balance with unbalanced temperaments running amok. So God has planned for opposites to attract each other in order to keep his race in balance. This is fine for God, but it is rough on us! Thus we find ourselves attracted to, in love with, and finally married to someone of precisely opposite ways of reacting to life.

Irma and I both loved our children dearly, but one

expressed this love through strict discipline, the other by means of an easygoing relationship. We both want security—but one by saving, the other by investing. We both want release from tension—but one of us through withdrawal, the other through conversation. We may have identical goals, but the methods by which we pursue them are diametrically opposite. What to do?

The first thing is to recognize and admit these differences. "My mate has a different temperament than I have and meets situations and problems in a different way than I do." For instance, Irma tends to explode; I am apt to withdraw. She likes to hang on to money and save it. I want to invest it and take risks. Let us then frankly admit these differences in taste and temperament.

In the second place, we need to set our mate free to be the kind of a person he or she is, to act and respond in the way that seems appropriate. It would seem Jesus recognized the different temperaments of his disciples: Simon Peter, the impetuous; John, emotionally volatile. But Jesus did not seek to change their personalities. Rather he sought to change the direction and manner in which these temperaments functioned. Peter is still impetuous after Pentecost, but there is a change in the very center of his being. John, who would call down fire on the Samaritans, now writes of the love of God. His emotions are still dominant but they move in a different direction.

It is our task not to try and change the kind of mate 

that each of us has, but to become enablers, thus affirming the spouse's personhood as each seeks to grow into a more loving and effective partner.

After we have recognized these differences and have set our mates free to be the persons they are (perhaps not wanting to go to church, disciplining the children too severely, or going critically over the grocery slip when you come back with bags of provisions), then comes the third step: the challenge to love them as they are and not to try and change them.

How skilled Jesus was in this art! When he first called Simon he knew him to be undependable and boastful; yet he envisioned in him such rocklike qualities that he dared to call him Simon *Peter* (a rock). Simon Peter frequently failed Jesus, disappointed him, and even denied him; yet Jesus continued to have faith in the Peter who was to be and meanwhile kept loving the Simon who was.

Can we do that with our mates? Dream dreams of what they may become, believe in these dreams for them, and yet rejoice in and love what they are here and now? Can we believe in the Peter who is to be in our partners and yet still love the Simon who is?

Fourth, can we go 100 percent of the way in seeking to meet the limitations and handicaps of our partners? Bill liked to sail. After marriage he bought a boat and asked Alice to go sailing with him. She tried hard to be a good sailor and share Bill's enthusiasm. But each trip found her petrified with fear. Bill's love for Alice prompted him to reevaluate his recreation plans and give up sailing. Together they decided on camping, something they both enjoyed. For years they were avid campers, spending much time together in woodlands and mountains. Bill could have insisted on boating—either going alone or insisting Alice go along—which would not have been the way of love. "Love does not insist on its own way" (I Corinthians 13:5). He could have reluctantly given up his boating, holding a resentment. He chose, however, of his own free will to discover a shared experience that would be fun for both.

In other instances one partner may not want to change at first, but love enables each gradually to grow toward the other. The timid one will slowly learn to risk, the forthright one will learn some caution. The frugal one will move toward spending, and the free soul will practice some restraint. When we were first married and heavily in debt I wanted to hear symphonies. If Irma had had her way, we would not have gone to concerts until we were out of debt. If I had had my way we would have gone too often. Each of us gave a little, and we found a happy medium, which we believed to be God's plan for us.

When God draws opposites into a marriage, he brings together persons with complementary traits. Thoughtfulness is balanced with impetuosity, quietness with explosiveness, restraint with plunging. Continuing love and discipline can so unite these opposing halves that day by day they grow into a unified whole. Each is forever different, yet both are forever rooted more closely together in a common and deepening fellowship.

# CHAPTER TWO

# Interaction

Love is not love which alters
When it alteration finds.

—*William Shakespeare*

Irma and I have a long-established custom that she puts her letters ready for mailing on the top right hand corner of her desk. When I am ready to go to the post office I pick up my mail, walk through the room where her desk is, pick up her mail, and proceed on my errand. Once in a while she hears me start from my room and calls out, "Don't forget my mail." My hand may at that very moment be stretched out and in the act of picking up her letters.

Yet, on hearing those words, there is suddenly something perverse in me that resists, and I find I do not want to gather up those letters. As long as it was my idea to mail her letters, that's fine! But when she asks me to do it, I resist.

Now I know full well that I sometimes forget her letters. I have been known more than once to walk right by them. So I know that I often need to be told! Then what is it in me that, even though I know I need to be reminded, causes me to resist when I am directed? We can call it Original Sin, the perversity of human nature, or the simple desire to have one's own way and run one's own life.

It is wise to recognize this trait in human nature both in ourselves and in others and to plan our encounters accordingly. People like to be given the privilege of decision-making rather than being told what to do. Therefore it is wise to impart information rather than give a command. If Irma says, "My letter to Aunt Sue or my note to renew our subscription to the *Herald* is on my desk," this honors me with decision-making and I can respond affirmatively. The directive, "The gas is low, you'd better stop at Bernie's and fill up before you start," is harder for me to take than a simple statement that advises me of the situation but gives no advice, such as, "I noticed the gas was low when I drove in last night, sorry I didn't fill it for you." A statement is much easier to live with than a flat command or piece of advice.

Our tendency to direct our partners can arise from our desire to avoid the pain and growth process of living with opposites. It suggests that we know better than the other person what should be done and how. It also limits the growth possibilities in our mate: the opportunities for trial and error and decision-making in the other person.

If we use argument and command or pleading and tears to change our mate's mind, we often build up an inner resistance so that the new course of action is adopted with reluctance or with a divided will. We can win an argument and lose some of the friendship. We change people's behavior at the risk of losing their inner good will.

It may be that our desire to direct our partner may be rooted in a desire to play God and to be in control. It is the old power play where one person likes to be number one and make the decisions. Sometimes I can try to be subtle about it and let Irma make the decisions in 90 percent of the situations, while insisting on getting my way in the 10 percent I really care about.

Sometimes my desire to direct or control is rooted in sheer egotism. I think my way is best and right. I want my wife and children to be duplicates of me. I am insensitive to the fact that God has implanted within them unique and beautiful personalities. Rather than affirm and love them so that they will develop along the lines that God has planned, I seek to force them into a mold of my own choosing.

Margaret came to me angry because her husband and children no longer respected her or responded to her wishes. In a short time we discovered that her mother had been a strong person who controlled everyone in the house. When Margaret became a teen-ager this control became almost intolerable, but she repressed her anger, inwardly resolving to take control some day in her own home. This she has done with disastrous results. We talked awhile. Soon she was asking God to take away the desire to control and to help her set her family free. Slowly a new comaraderie and joy entered that home.

Another reason to want to direct people, whether in the home or outside it, is to spare myself trouble. Life would be so much easier for me if everyone would be on time and thoughtful and live up to their promises and do things my way. Yes, my life would be easier for the moment, but it would deny the opportunities for growth and for direct encounter both to myself and my partner.

It is really quite insane trying to change people by frontal attack—scolding, nagging, threatening, advising, pleading. The more we try to change people, the more we arouse resistance, overt or hidden. I recognize in myself a kind of primordial cussedness that refuses to be told what to do. In the same way argument often serves to make other persons bolster their positions more firmly, and we end up further apart than when we started. Or there may be outward compliance and inner reservation or resentment.

Here are some specific steps that have proved helpful in our marriage:

*1.* Recognize and admit differences between each other.

*2.* Set each other free, mutually to grow and develop into the person God has planned. Thank God for each other and love each other as you are today without waiting for change or growth.

*3.* Affirm each other. Enhance and do not diminish or downgrade. Find things in each other to admire and verbally praise. Be slow to undermine and blame, quick to affirm and build up.

*4.* There needs always to be an opportunity for person-to-person conversation in every home. Plan times of honest and loving encounter when each can share the several places of loneliness, hurt, and need. It is advisable not to have this encounter when you are hurt or angry and the emotions are raw and painful. Wait if at all possible a few hours or even a few days. Choose a time of closeness and fellowship or let one of you specifically request a time for a heart-to-heart talk, even though the other may not feel like it at that moment. Let each strive to meet the other's need, setting a time and place, having an inner mood of readiness to listen and a desire to build a closer relationship.

*5.* Then as far as possible do not point out the *other's* faults and sin, but share *your* own faults, *your* needs, and *your* places of hurt. Leave it to God's Spirit to prompt your partner to speak of his faults. With most couples one of the two will speak up first and more easily. The other may be slower to share; it may even be hours or days before there is a response. If at all possible, set your partner free to make his or her own decision and to speak when ready, so that the response comes voluntarily from within and is not forced or cajoled.

It may be right to come back to the problem from time to time. But avoid debating language, nagging, scolding or ultimatums. Be willing to restate the hurts and needs on a feeling level and not in an accusatory manner. Be patient. Recall how long and patiently Jesus waited for his disciples to change and grow. Recall how long God is still waiting for each of us to change. Be patient!

6. If one of the partners refuses to cooperate or to listen and to respond to the overture, then let the one who has taken the initiative of love continue to be loving, self-sacrificing, and yet buoyed up by a strong faith for the partner. This is what Calvary is all about—a God who through Jesus makes an overture of love. Humankind refuses to respond, but God keeps on loving, waiting, and believing. To love not just to get results but for the sheer joy of loving is to model God's kind of love in our marriages.

*Author's Note:* This chapter reveals my personal bias against being directed. I resisted it as a little child; I rebelled against it as an adolescent. I have had to wrestle with it through sixty-five years of marriage. Only last week I took the matter to God in prayer, and he gave me the verse, Acts 9:6*b*, "You will be told what you are to do"! I frequently forget, I often make mistakes. So I need to be directed, and yet there are times when I still find myself resenting direction. How patient God and people have been with me!

# CHAPTER THREE

# Affirmation and Praise

Sometimes I sit back and wonder what would have happened to me if I hadn't met Gracie. I wonder if I would have made it!

*—George Burns*

"Did you see anything different in the dining room?" my wife asked. I had just returned from an out-of-town engagement and had walked right through the dining room to greet Irma in the kitchen. It was a warm, sunny day and Irma had given the dining room a spring cleaning.

"No," I replied.

She went with me into that room and pointed, "I

polished the furniture, waxed the floor, washed and ironed the curtains—don't you see any difference?"

My glance wandered to the windows, smudged with fingerprints. "Did you wash the windows?" She broke into tears, and I stood there mystified.

She had worked all day on that room, with two small children running in and out demanding her attention. By late afternoon she was too tired to do any more. As soon as I had spoken I was filled with shame. I realized that I had singled out the one thing she had not done, and had failed to praise her for any of the good things she had done.

The incident made a deep impression on me in those early years of marriage. As I reflected on it in the days that followed, I found out a few things about myself. When I was a small boy, my father had scrutinized my work to find faults that he might correct. Now, I was walking in my father's footsteps, seeking to find fault with my wife's housekeeping. Moreover, I recognized in myself a desire to be top dog in my home. I realized that I was forming a habit of pushing Irma down in an effort to pull myself up. It was a subtle way of playing the power game.

Then I also discovered something in myself that I did not like. I possessed a sadistic pleasure in withholding approval and finding fault. I refused to accept this truth for weeks. But there it was. If there was nothing with which to find fault, I discovered I could use the weapon of silence! I would rather find fault than praise. I would come home tired from a church event or trip and be as silent as a clam when Irma was so eager to know what had happened. I kidded myself into thinking I was an introvert and found it hard to express myself. But I found no trouble in talking about things in which I was interested. Why not the things in which she was interested?

God was trying to show me that I was replaying my childhood tapes of years gone by. As a child I had been downgraded by my parents. When the school report card came, my parents had scolded me for B's and C's but never praised me for A's. My father would say, "If there's a wrong way of doing a thing you'll find it." Now a score of years later I was discovering that I was conditioning myself to respond to negative stimuli and to be unaware of the positive ones. My wife would serve a nice meal, and I could eat it in silence. But if one of the articles of food was too salty or burned a little, how quickly I would remark on it. I could see and speak of the unwashed windows while maintaining a stony silence about the many lovely things she had done in that room.

Recently in a supermarket my wife saw a little boy helping his mother transfer the groceries from the cart to the counter. In a derisive voice the mother said to the clerk, "He'll drop it; I know he'll drop it." A few weeks later in the same store she saw another little fellow helping his mother and this time heard the words: "He's mother's helper. I just don't know what I'd do without him." One is just as easy to say as the other.

How often a group of women will discuss their husbands at a coffee klatch or social event—he's always late, careless, demanding, never picks up his clothes, just will not do those chores around the house! Men also can be very cruel as they discuss their wives, sometimes revealing intimacies that should never be mentioned beyond the home. A safe rule is: never put down your mate whether talking to or talking about him or her.

Sometimes we use humor as a putdown thinking it does not hurt; but jokes made at the other's expense, especially in areas where we are sensitive—cooking, driving, providing, appearance—can cause deep and lasting pain. A smile may camouflage the throwing of the dart, but venom is there that can destroy a healthy marriage.

Men and women alike return home from work tired and exhausted. Egos have been bruised. Critical or ill-tempered words from the boss or a disgruntled customer or employee have left open wounds. How important are the first words we hear when we enter the house! When children come home from school or play, how do we greet them? "Hurry up! I have to take you to the dentist." "Now get your homework done before you go out to play"; or "I'm so glad to see you. I've been waiting ever since you left this morning, wanting to see you back. Did you have a good day? Tell me what happened."

What proportion of your comments to your spouse or children are negative rather than positive?

Do you affirm and enhance more often than diminish and tear down? Do you seek to immerse yourself in their interests, or do you try to fit people into your plans and wishes?

The Bible frequently speaks of praise and giving thanks. These are skills that require cultivation. Affirmation is not a gift but a quality of life that can be developed. I had been married over ten years before I put my nose into a batch of clean laundry one day and told my wife how sweet it smelled and thanked her for washing my clothes. I was amazed that I had simply taken this task of hers for granted all these years. Yet if by any chance there was no clean shirt or underwear on hand I could easily speak up.

God finally got me to the place where I consciously sought to find opportunities when I could affirm and praise Irma. Slowly I learned to overlook the places where she might have slipped up. Now for over half a century we have been growing in the art of affirming and undergirding each other. Three or four years ago, with both of us in our eighties, we found that we were misplacing and dropping things more frequently. After one such little accident when something fell to the floor and broke we both spoke together, "I guess we'll just have to accept the fact that these things will happen." There was a very comfortable feeling, each knowing that the other understood and that there was mutual support for the other regardless of what we might do.

I find that a little time spent with God and with

the spirit of Christ dramatically changes my attitude toward Irma. When I see myself as a sinner loved and forgiven of God, I find I am no longer judgmental and fault-finding. I discover a new appreciation and reverence for each member of my family. More and more the members of my family appear to me as precious gifts of God, to be honored and affirmed. More and more I become an affirmer and an enabler helping them become the persons God intended them to be.

Out of this new appreciation and reverence has sprung gratitude and joy for my family. I can always tell when I am slipping away from this attitude. I may come home tired and in my fatigue thinking of no one but myself. My first four sentences are apt to be, "Are there any messages? Is there any mail? How long will supper be? I have to go out tonight." Every one of these sentences is self-centered and directed toward my interests only. I am oblivious of the fact that my wife may have had a hard day. I overlook the fact that she, like me, is a person in need of recognition, of warmth, and of affirmation.

Nearly fifty years ago God showed me how self-centered this kind of behavior was, and I vowed that no matter how fatigued I might be I would never come home again without my primary thought being of those who were in the home that I was entering. I started the habit of stopping my car a few blocks from home. I thanked God for the wife and children I was about to see. I asked him to give me a joyous spirit and the grace to forget about myself and my fatigue. Invariably I experienced an inrushing of both physical and spiritual strength. Life took on a new excitement for me. I was eager to enter the house not to rest because I was tired, or to eat at once because I had an appointment. I was eager to see the wife and children whom God had given me. I entered into their interests, their joys and frustrations and became one with them, instead of centering in on myself.

This new center of living led to many exciting innovations. I took time to play golf and climb the White Mountains with the children. I found time for eating out and pleasure trips with my wife. There was a new camaraderie among us. The drive for discipline and order was supplanted by fellowship and joy. I learned to become a friend of my children and a pal to my wife. Happy little surprises multiplied. On one occasion I was leaving for a week's speaking tour. Unbeknown to her, I took seven three-by-five cards, wrote a brief love note on each, and hid them: one under her pillow, another in the dirty clothes hamper, a third in the refrigerator, a fourth by one of the clocks, and so on. I even opened a new half-gallon of her favorite ice cream and plastered one of the cards there, carefully closing the cover again so it would retain its innocent look. She talked of that for weeks, and how we laughed as she narrated her treasure hunt!

# CHAPTER FOUR

# The Round Table

Bring the full tithes into the storehouse, that there may be food in my house; and thereby put me to the test, says the Lord of hosts, if I will not open the windows of heaven for you and pour down for you an overflowing blessing."

—*Malachi 3:10*

There came a time in our home life when I saw that God wanted a hand in our family finances. It was the day my semi-monthly salary check came from the church. I was serving as minister, and the thought bore in on me that this was not my money, but God's. It was given not to me personally but to the entire family to steward and use on his behalf.

I called the family together about an old round table. I placed the check in the center of the table and said: "Until today I have always thought of this check as being something I earned and therefore as mine to spend or dole out as I wished. Today, however, God is showing me that it is not my money. He has given it not just to me, but to all of us to steward according to his plans for us."

One of the boys, who had read the story of the Knights of the Round Table, had suggested the name "Round Table" for our old family table because we sat there as equals. Each felt free to speak honestly and openly. Each knew he or she was listened to and respected. God was the head of this table, and the five of us sat together as his children; two boys twelve and sixteen, a girl ten, my wife, and I.

Until now I had been keeping a tight rein on the family money, trying to get the children to keep their allowances down, trying to pay off the family debts. But I was more free with the amount of money I spent on books for my library, an amount that Irma thought to be much too large. But a man seldom hears the word of the Lord when it is spoken by his wife, so I went on my merry way buying whatever books I fancied.

We were heavily in debt. I had assumed part of my brother's funeral expenses and debts. There were doctors' and dentists' bills, car payments, and notes falling due at the bank. My wife and I had even discussed giving up tithing until we got out of debt. As we sat around the table I spoke in detail of the family finances, letting my wife and children know for the first time the exact amount of our resources and obligations. I passed out pencils and paper to each and said, "Let us ask God what is his will for this money, how it should be stewarded and spent." There were a few minutes of silence and then pencils began to move.

The first item on each of the three children's papers was the tithe. My wife and I didn't stand a chance of discontinuing that! Each of the young people volunteered to take a smaller allowance. My wife, always frugal, saw where she could save. Suggestions to turn off lights and conserve fuel came from all of us. God finally got to me on my careless expenditure of money for books, and I freely admitted that my wife had been right in this.

The result of this interchange with regard to finances, meant a closer bond in the family. My wife and the children felt trusted and honored that trust. All five of us had a new motivation toward a wiser stewarding of the family resources. It became a very natural procedure to discuss any important expenditures with the entire family. The young folks took this responsibility seriously and kept confidential these items of family interest.

Money can be a frequent source of conflict between husband and wife. It is unwise to use money as a reward or a punishment with spouse or children. A well-to-do friend of mine put a five-hundred-dollar check under his wife's plate at dinner on her birthday. Later she told me, "I would gladly forego all his gifts of money if only he would take time personally to select and buy a gift or touch me in tenderness once in a while."

Money can be a beautiful gift if it comes from a loving heart, but it can also be a cop-out, a salve to compensate for our giving so little of our time and ourselves to our loved ones. As such it can be brutally unkind, doubly so because it appears so generous. Money can be used as a weapon of power: we may imply in our giving, "I earned this money, therefore I should have the say as to how it is spent." The selfish withholding of money from a partner, like the selfish withholding of sex, can be a cruel form of the power play in a home. No wonder Jesus taught that the grasping of money could keep us from radiant life in God's kingdom.

Happy is that family that sees money and all of life's blessings as gifts from God to be stewarded under his leading.

Tithing can be a spiritual adventure. It can introduce a couple to a new plateau of living. When we give the first tenth of our income to the Lord it helps set the priorities of our lives. Paul prays that the Philippians may have "a sense of what is vital" (Philippians 1:10 Moffatt). Planning the first tenth for God invariably means that the other nine-tenths are stewarded more wisely, and the amazing miracle happens in home after home that tithers are blessed not only spiritually but financially. We don't do it for financial gain. That is to deny God and the primacy of love. We do it because our hearts overflow with gratitude. Then God sees to it that "all these things shall be yours as well" (Matthew 6:33), in abundance.

God widens the sympathies and pushes back the spiritual horizons of those who commit their financial decisions to him. The conversation and prayers at the table reach to the corners of the earth. Unexpected returns are forever pouring into the home. Life is full of surprises. God is true to his Word. He pours down overflowing blessings. Today our government and many citizens are guilty of irresponsible spending, prodigal use of our nation's resources, thus mortgaging the lives and fortunes of unborn generations. Our witness can be a faithful stewarding of money and the resources of God's world as we live lives of financial integrity and responsibility.

# Love Without Limit

Love never ends.

*—1 Corinthians 13:8a*

My wife and I go to the supermarket together. My part is to be chauffeur and read while she shops. She likes to shop alone, browsing, picking up items on special sale, and generally enjoying herself.

As Irma leaves the car I frequently ask how long she will be. "Thirty minutes," she may say. I am content to wait for I have a book and settle down to read, keeping an occasional eye on the store exit so as not to keep her waiting. After a while I chance to look at my watch. Thirty-five minutes have gone by! She has overstayed the thirty-minute agreement. I get uptight. "What is she doing? Why does she take so long?" I had love enough for thirty minutes, but not for thirty-five!

What is this self-will in me that measures out kindness? Why am I willing to love only if other people behave within the limits that I have set for them?

Too often we tend to relate to one another on a calculated kindness level. We sense one another's level of tolerance or "boiling point" and reply with just enough kindliness to keep peace and soothe raw nerves. When the spouse's voice reaches a certain pitch we start to cooperate. After six weeks of being reminded about putting up those hooks in the cupboard, it's time to act! We have trained ourselves to respond with calculated good will so as to keep a tolerable degree of peace. We lubricate with just enough oil of helpfulness to keep things running smoothly.

I believe the Spirit of Christ wants to place us on a different level than this—one of love without limit. When the freshness and fullness of marriage begin to wear off we run for cover and begin to be extra kind, extra careful with each other in order to ensure a good marriage and a sweet, peaceful home for the children. When problems of difference in temperaments, viewpoints, and decision-making raise their heads, again we tend to cop out. Sometimes we pretend the problems are not there. Other times we divide areas of responsibility, often by conventional sex roles; the husband, for instance, cares for the finances, car, and vacation plans, and the wife sees to the home, and cares for the children, meals, and garden. We are apt to think that if we divide the decision-making there will be fewer arguments and that will be better for the children. In such a climate we begin to have doubts about the future of our marriage. We try to be kind and sweet, and above all avoid touchy or troublesome subjects.

Some couples, instead of going the sweetness or kindness route, will try arguing and quarreling. We explode with words that sting, barbed phrases that hurt for days or months to come. There is a place for anger, but if we do get angry let us learn how to deal with it instead of venting it on the one we love (see chapter 10).

Why settle for the ways of either quarreling or calculated kindness? Why must we develop skills of steering away from rough waters? Even as Jacob and the Angel wrestled (Genesis 33:24-28) so also couples are meant to be passionately in love and yet to wrestle together. Through pain and growth they discover deeper and more mature ways of living and loving. It is better parenting for children to be brought up in a home where parents talk through and wrestle together with the problems of life. For them also life is going to be a struggle, and the memory of parents wrestling with decision-making will in turn strengthen their marriage.

My wife and I differ radically on the use and expenditure of money. Yet come what may, we are thoroughly committed to love each other. Each of us is determined not to take advantage of the other's good nature and plead for his or her way. We still talk, discuss, honor each other's opinions and judgments. We end up making the decision that we both think is right under the circumstances—often not what both or even either would like, but what seems right to us at the time.

We are not afraid to differ, to state what we feel. We don't need to fight for our positions or try to impress each other. We know each listens and values the words of the other. We can speak, knowing we are heard. We can afford to let a decision be tentative and less than perfect because we know our task is not to arrive at the right answer. Our task is to let our love for each other guide the process of dialogue and conclusion. The final decision is not as important as the means by which we have arrived at our conclusion.

We read in the life of Jesus how he walked with his disciples over the rough and rocky roads of their doubts, disbeliefs, quarrelings, and even desertion. It was not easy for Jesus. He said to his disciples on different occasions, "How long am I to bear with you?" . . . "Could you not watch with me one hour?" . . . "Get thee behind me, Satan." . . . "O ye of little faith." But he never swerved in his commitment to be loyal to them and to love them. He so believed in them that they later became stalwart pillars of the Christian church with its glorious history of pilgrims and martyrs.

So why should we couples with love in our hearts settle for anything less than a passionate, unswerving devotion to each other? It is within the bonds of such devotion that we think and talk through our problems and differences with listening and caring. We proceed with patience and gentleness, knowing that the process is the reward. The means by which we arrive is indeed the goal.

Bill and Alice sat down to talk. Bill admitted that all his wife had said was true. He was careless: he seldom put the cover on the toothpaste or closed the toilet cover. Often he failed to clean out the litter in the car when he took Alice for a ride. The newspaper was a shambles when he got through with it.

Alice spoke of her desire for a neat house and the continuing battle to get the children to keep their rooms neat and not leave things around the house. There was the impasse.

Then each began to move toward the other. Bill had a demanding job—computers, figures, pages of statistics. He spoke of the strain under which he worked and the fear that he might crack up. His father, he recalled, had had a breakdown at about his age. Coming home was letting down. Yet he knew he shouldn't be oblivious to Alice's wishes for a neat house. Alice in turn spoke of her childhood training in neatness, her fears that the children would not turn out well, her feeling of frustration at ending each day with so much undone and the house never picked up.



The impasse was still there, but this time each

was thinking not so much of self and the desire to have one's own way. Each was seeing life from the other's viewpoint, camping as it were on the other's turf. Soon there were glances of recognition, of sympathy, of love. Arms went around each other. The problems were still there. The car would be littered sometimes, the paper scattered; but Alice knew that Bill cared and that he would try. Bill knew that Alice had walked a few steps into his heart and had loved what she had seen. The problems were small now. The love was great. The talk had become a tryst. Love was without limit.

# CHAPTER SIX

# *Living by Dreams*

Mine is the sunlight!
Mine is the morning.
Born of the one light
Eden saw play!
Praise with elation,
Praise every morning,
God's re-creation
Of the new day!

—*Eleanor Farjeon*

From the very beginning the marriage was under a handicap. The groom's mother had given them as a wedding present a house completely furnished from living room and bedrooms to even landscaping and flower beds. This couple was robbed of the excitement of planning, the tension of struggle, the testing of their faith in themselves and God. They were denied the privilege of dreaming their own dreams and the shared and exciting struggle to fulfill them. Thus they were also denied the joy of meeting and overcoming hardships—the healthy leanness which breeds strength of spirit.

I contrast this with a couple who took all their meager savings to make a down payment on an old farmhouse and moved into the one habitable room. When we called there months later we saw the home in the process of being renovated. A partition had been torn out here, but a sketch of the room that was to be had been attached to the wall. In the bathroom, still with only a curtain for a door, a tile and a few square inches of wallpaper were glued to the wall, thus placing their dreams before them. Room after room had a piece of wallpaper, a swatch of carpet, a splash or two of color. They dreamed, they worked, they grew. Now, thirty years later, the fulfilled dream includes not only the restored house but also poignant and precious memories of shared experiences through the years.

Never were there better days for dreams than today. Some young people are defeated before they start. "We don't plan to have children." "They will only be killed in a nuclear war." "The world is overpopulated, underfed." "This is no place to bring up kids." These dark days are just the times in which to dream—more than ever! The darker the night, the brighter the stars. The darkness yields to the radiant morn.

Jesus was born in the Middle East. What a hopeless moral climate there is with the Israelis, the Arabs, and the PLO quarreling and killing. But go back two thousand years, and the bitterness and hatreds were even worse—Samaritans, Romans, Jews, collaborators, underground rebels! These hostilities caused Jesus to be nailed on the cross. In spite of this hotbed of hate and intrigue, Jesus dared to dream the greatest of dreams—the coming of the kingdom of God. He dared to envision a bond of unbreakable love between persons of different races and ethnic backgrounds. He dreamed of "peace on earth and good will among men."

Every couple that dreams of love where there has been no love, of community where people have merely existed in isolation, walks where Jesus walked, dreams as he dreamed, and believes as he believed. Their task is to build their little corner of the kingdom of God in spite of the odds that are against them, modeling the love and oneness as Jesus modeled it first with his Father and then with his fellow man.

Each home is a venture of faith, flying a flag in defiance of a world that looks askance at idealism, sacrificial love, and long-term commitments. A family is a miniature kingdom of God set in the midst of doubting people. Establishing a new home is a venture of faith, a new opportunity to live out the dream two lovers dared to dream when first they fell in love.

Eleanor Farjeon, in the foregoing poem, sees each new day as the reenactment of that primal joy that burst forth at Creation when God said, "It was good!" What the poet sees happening as she greets each morning, you and I can see taking place in our homes with each new day. Every day there can be a reenactment of the love that drew us together as we dated, of the joy of that first moment when we knew we were made for each other, of the light in our eyes as we took our vows. The miracle of the love that God gives us is its unending flow and ever deepening enrichment.

Let each morning's greeting and embrace have something of that moment when love first broke through. Express your need of each other. Yet how we hesitate to let even our loved ones know of our inner hurts and inadequacies! At one of our retreats a woman said, "It takes a lot of guts for a wife to tell her husband that she needs him and wants to love him more, but that she doesn't know how." Yet saying this opened the wellsprings for them both. The husband saw deep in the heart of his mate the dream she cherished and her struggle to make it a reality. His response was a new tenderness and openness.

In varied, spontaneous, and joyous ways speak of your needs and rejoice in that fact that you have each other. Put your love into words. Say it out loud in different ways and places! Thank God for each other privately in your own hearts and audibly in each other's presence. Say it in word, touch, smile, surprise—a variety of languages!

Daily give of yourself to make possible the fulfillment and growth of your mate. So love that you each feel loved, so listen that each feels heard, so support that each feels strengthened. Forget yourself; live for your partner and trust your partner's response. That may come right away, or it may be weeks or even years later. Keep loving, keep believing, keep trusting. Within you is the love of God that forever gives of itself, knowing that ultimately humankind will respond and return that love. You also can afford to wait and love, for selfless love is the greatest power on earth.

CHAPTER SEVEN

# Open Hearts

Open your hearts to us.

—*II Corinthians* 7:2a

All of us live within the tension of wanting and yet dreading to be known. We long to share, and yet we treasure our privacy. The single person laments, "I miss having someone to talk things over with when I come home at night." And the same person adds, "Sometimes it's good not to have to feel accountable, just to be able to keep things to myself." We all both welcome and dread being known.

The story is told of a pack of porcupines marooned

on an icy plain one bitter cold, sub-zero night. As the wind increased and the temperature fell the animals moved closer together for body warmth. The more they huddled, the more the quills of the contacting porcupines began to hurt. The closer they moved, the greater the pain! A few of them decided they could stand the discomfort no longer, so they went apart separately and slept alone. When morning came, those that had gone off by themselves were frozen and dead, but those in the pack survived.

It is enticing, but costly, to become known. We begin sharing our little secrets as we date and fall in love. But soon we fear we may have revealed too much. Our mate knows so much about us that we feel threatened. Some of us fear being hurt, so we do not trust deeply or share intimately. We keep whole areas of our lives to ourselves. Thus we avoid much pain, but in so doing we deny ourselves possibilities of richer and more rewarding relationships.

Jesus lived a life of intimacy. He shared such a closeness with God that he could say, "I and the Father are one" (John 10:30). He opened his heart to his disciples as rapidly as they were able to receive his confidences ("I have yet many things to say to you, but you cannot bear them now"—John 16:12). He continued to be transparent with his disciples even though they doubted and misunderstood his words. He opened his heart to his enemies, though they were to use his words against him as they sought to kill him. Intimacy was his pattern of life.

Intimacy in marriage is a willingness so to trust ourselves to another that there can be no withdrawal, no face-saving, no alternative way out. We open our hearts to the depths. We trust the very core of our being to the one we love. We seek to imitate Jesus' quality of transparency that knew no limits. Marriage is a day-by-day growth in this kind of living. All that we are we trust to our partner, and after sixty-five years Irma and I are still working at it!

I recall writing a letter to my son some years ago. It was not just a regular newsy letter, but one in which I opened my heart, sharing defeats and dreams, failures and victories. As I started to fold the letter, the thought came to me, "Share this letter with Irma before you mail it." But I went on folding it and started to put it in the envelope. Again the thought, "Share it with Irma." I pushed the letter further into the envelope and raised it to my lips to seal it. Still the thought persisted, "Let Irma read it." And so, finally, just before I sealed it, I took it out and carried it into the next room to let Irma read it. God won! Now there might well be situations where a father and son have reasons for a privacy that admits no one else, but in this case I knew full well that letting Irma read this letter would mean placing myself in a situation where I would have to live with the person who knew these things about me. My son lived a thousand miles away, and we saw each other once a year. But now I would be sitting at the table two or three times a day with the one who knew these things, someone who might remind me of them, let me know when I failed to live up to them.

Yes, there have been times when Irma and I have turned these confidences into weapons and used them against each other, even as the religious leaders of Jesus' time used his confidences about his father against him. I have reminded Irma of her failures so as to be one up on her. I have thrown up to her the times she has not lived up to the dreams she has shared. The beast in me rears its head every once in a while, and I do things and say things that hurt. Later I regret this deeply. My heart is a battlefield. I know what it is to have a real struggle within myself, to allow the best in me to be overcome by the worst; and also, thank God, to have the worst in me overcome by the best. Through the years we are growing together, for each of us lives within the other.

More and more we have come to see that a deep opening of heart between us is giving each of us the opportunity to walk into the very inner sanctum of the other's being, to walk into the innermost holy of holies. More and more we come to honor and respect that privilege as one of the choice gifts of marriage. We are custodians, keepers of each other's hearts and secrets. We treasure them with tenderness and fidelity. There is always a risk when one is dealing with priceless treasures. But we who trust in the open way of life still prefer to take that risk.



Irma and I can now look back on our growth

through the years. Fifty years ago when I told Irma of a misdeed or a failure to live up to the highest, she said, "Oh, Lee, how could you!" and followed that sentence with, "Now if I had been you I would have . . ." Those words hurt! Inwardly I would resolve never to open my heart to her again. But I was committed to the "way of the open heart," and so I chose to continue to share my weaknesses and needs, my dreams and my hopes. For many years now when I have shared some painful incident her reply has been something like, "Lee, the more I know about you the more I love you." The perfect response! It affirms me, empowers me, and makes me want to communicate on an even deeper level. This quality of intimacy reflects the very nature of love as we know it in Jesus—a love that must by its very nature keep on giving and sharing itself.

John earned small pay. For years he plodded on faithfully, with no promotions and few financial rewards. He had frequently told Joan that he was sorry he was not earning more for her and the kids. But one day he opened his heart in depth and shared his feeling of inadequacy. He could not provide for Joan the things that all her friends enjoyed. There was hurt and pain. But Joan responded with: "John, you give me yourself and that's worth more than all the things you might provide. I am a rich woman to have a love like yours. My children, our children, are blessed beyond measure to have a father like you."

Partners who live like this find a listening ear and an understanding heart as they come to each other after a financial setback, a traumatic operation, a silly social faux pas, or a lapse of fidelity. Together they begin again.

# Giving Thanks

I will not enter my house
or get into my bed;
I will not give sleep to my eyes
or slumber to my eyelids,
until I find place for the Lord.

—*Psalm 132:3-5*a

God has given us this love that is ours. He has given us strength to work and a zest for living. He has given us the family with whom we eat. Yet many families never thank him at all. Others mumble some routine phrases. In others, parents ask one of the children to "say grace." We would not treat a fellow human being like that. If friends of ours provided a place of rest for us, food to eat, and company with whom to chat, how quickly we would voice our thanks to them. Should we not give thanks to God with equal enthusiasm?

Yet grace at table is often a perfunctory repetition of the same words day after day, an empty ritual accompanied with little or no feeling. Indeed we can eat meal after meal, year after year, and never verbalize our thanks.

Most of us are somewhat tongue-tied and self-conscious when it comes to thinking of new and genuine ways of giving thanks. But surely God's goodness is such as to warrant a vibrant expression of gratitude.

When you give thanks, use memorized poems or prayers sparingly; they soon lose their forcefulness. Talk simply to God as you would to a human host, giving thanks, expressing joy and appreciation. Include not only the meal, but some of the day's events in your gratitude. Rotate the praying, letting a different person pray at each meal.

Vary the style. Sometimes when I come to the table a few seconds late and Irma is already seated, I stand behind her, put my arms around her, and thank God in that position with a kiss on the top of her head for the amen. Holding hands or touching hands adds variety. Each one's mentioning one item for which he or she is particularly grateful that day adds another dimension. Sometimes one member has a story (short, we hope!) to tell, or a little trophy to exhibit.

On occasion I have taken a piece of bread or toast and broken off a piece for Irma and then one for myself, saying something like: "Here we are, our lives all being given to each other, broken for each other, and yet always made whole. Thank you, God, for one another."

A song, a hymn, a verse of a poem can add variety. It is not necessary to have novelty just for novelty's sake. But a little thought and preparation can help make this shared experience of giving thanks at meal times a significant part of the family life.

This God who is in our marriage delights to be included in our joys and to be thanked for our blessings. How quickly we turn to him for help if dire problems arise; how easy to blame him when something goes wrong! Why not cultivate the habit of thanking him in natural, everyday language for the happy surprises and continuing stream of good gifts that come to us?

When we travel by car, how natural it is to pull over to the side of the road when we see a scene of unusual beauty. Why not reach out then and there, touch hands and audibly thank God for his gifts—and even more for his presence. At night, to stand holding hands across a crib or to look out toward the glowing west and give thanks; in church to sit with an occasional touch of hands. All these are recognitions and affirmation of the eternal triangle of love—God (or Jesus), husband, and wife.

Anniversaries and birthdays offer other opportunities for thanksgiving. Often the church calendar is used to announce these events. The congregation joins in celebration as the minister offers a prayer of praise.

There are the prayers we offer in the quiet intimacies of our home. John has returned from a dangerous trip. A hurricane had threatened. Now he is safe at home and Mary says, "Let's thank God, John." A child is healed. A grown child has been married and the parents return home feeling the new emptiness. They sit reminiscing, talking over the years that their child has been under their roof, and then spontaneously break into audible thanks to God. At the Communion service they hold hands again and quietly thank God. Moments like these are priceless experiences.

What occasions of thanksgiving there are! Prayers of thanks for the friendship in dating, thanks for the engagement and pledging of love, thanks for the marriage, for the new home, the knowledge of conception, the birth, and the rich succession of events. Thanks for the times when someone has returned to health; thanks for innumerable blessings day by day. The most intimate prayer can well be before or after the sexual relationship; kneeling by the bedside before the conception of a planned child and thanking God for the miracle to be, or the prayer of love and dedication made in the quiet peace that follows sex while still in each other's arms. Welling up from the husband's heart are words like these: "Thank you, God, for Mary, for the children you have given us. Help me to love her more deeply, to be the husband to her that I want to be, to be the kind of father I dream of being." And Mary's reply: "God, how I thank you for Jim and my being the mother of our children. I love Jim and the children so much. Thank you, thank you, God."

CHAPTER NINE

# Rechanneling Unused Love

Use it, or lose it.

One day years ago I came home exuberant and happy. I was oblivious as to exactly what my wife was doing. I merely saw her standing at the kitchen counter. I came up on her almost unnoticed, putting my arms around her kissed her on the back of the neck. She lifted her hands out of the flour she was mixing for an apple pie and in decisive tones said, "Lee, don't kiss me in the kitchen!"

Whereupon I turned and walked out of the kitchen, inwardly thinking, "No, I'll not kiss you in the kitchen, and it will be a long while before I offer to kiss you anywhere."

What had happened to that bubbling, overflowing love? The energy that was love had reversed direction and was now the source of bitterness and hurt. I was discovering something I had not known about love, namely that love rejected and unused can turn sour.

Love is not a commodity that can be stored like honey in a jar just waiting to be used. It is energy and life-force that must find expression or it changes its character. Used love grows sweet and strong; unused it becomes bitter and even turns rancid.

Mary is waiting for the car. Jim promised to be home by four o'clock sharp and stay with the children while she keeps her doctor's appointment. Four o'clock, no Jim! Four-fifteen, four-thirty, still no Jim! Mary is fit to be tied! When Jim finally comes, she explodes. Once again love has turned to anger because it was denied its normal and expected avenue of expression.

Sometimes love is thwarted because the other person is obstinate, stuffy, or tired. Sometimes we are the ones who are stubborn or weary and are unwilling to be gracious or loving. Sometimes there is a strange awkwardness that blocks the flow of love. Although I have been married a long time, I still know this feeling of awkwardness. For example, I may be driving the car with my left hand. My right hand is free and is on the arm rest between us. Irma's hand is just a few inches away. The thought occurs to me to reach over and touch her hand. Now, of course, most of the time I do so easily. But sometimes there is resistance, a self-consciousness, even a wondering if she would rather have me not touch her and tend to my driving. I know this is foolish and may even sound weird, but there it is. If I do not break through and act, there slowly builds up in me an inner mood of critical feelings and a defense mechanism as to why she does not want to be touched. Love, not acted upon, turns negative. What might have been good will becomes ill will.

How shall we process this anger? How shall we keep the love flowing? There is a story in the Gospels in which Jesus gives us a significant lesson. He had sent the disciples out two by two on a teaching-healing mission. They came back excited by what had happened, yet exhausted and in need of rest and infilling. Jesus said to them, "Come away by yourselves . . . and rest a while." Mark adds, "For many were coming and going, and they had no leisure even to eat" (6:31). Jesus had his loving plans all set: they would cross the lake to a lonely spot where they could rest and be restored in body and spirit. But other people interrupted those plans. A huge crowd ran around the southern tip of the lake and got there ahead of Jesus and the disciples, so that when they landed, instead of a lonely spot they found a crowded one. Jesus' plans for a quiet, restful time with his friends were blocked.

Since Jesus was tempted in all points as we are, he must have been tempted to be angry at those people for interfering with his plans. The unused love in him was about to turn sour! But we read: "He saw a great throng, and he had compassion on them, because they were like sheep without a shepherd; and he began to teach them many things." Later he fed them the loaves and fish.

Note these steps:

1. Jesus saw those who upset his plans in terms of their needs ("like sheep without a shepherd") and not their faults.

2. Jesus with nimbleness and flexibility changed his plans to fit the needs of those who had blocked him.

3. He did not withhold his love, but rechanneled it in another direction (teaching and feeding).

If Mary takes Jim's tardiness in this way, she will also keep the love flowing.

1. She sees Jim as having more work than he can handle, or as the victim of that forgetfulness that is part of his lovable nature. She focuses on his needs, not his faults.

2. She phones the doctor's office and asks if she can come late or have an appointment on another day, thus being flexible.

3. She meets Jim with a smile and a twinkle in her eye, "Honey, if I get to heaven before you I'll ask Peter not to close the door on you because you've kept him waiting." She has rechanneled her love.

When our opportunities to love or help a partner are denied to us, it is vital to our love flow that we sublimate and redirect its energies. Words of praise unuttered turn into feelings of criticism. Acts of kindness stifled and undone bring negative moods or actions.

When the children grow up and leave home we move into the empty-nest era. The children have formed the basis of much conversation and exciting adventure. Now they are gone. New areas of mutual interests must be found to ensure the love flow. One couple, childless for years, found their love changing to fault-finding and bickering. Humbly and honestly they faced what was happening. They adopted an eight-year-old orphan girl. The love flow began again.

One of the couples attending a summer conference had lost a seven-year-old daughter just eight weeks previous from infantile paralysis. Their tears were near the surface. Their hearts still ached, but they talked freely of their little girl. Some of us began to commiserate: "What a shame to have had her only those seven years. It's too bad you had to lose her so young." It was almost as if we were saying, "It would have been better not to have had her at all." The parents replied: "She brought us nothing but joy those seven years. Our lives and our home are inexpressibly richer for her having lived. We thank God for loaning her to us those seven years." The deep reserves of emotion within us can flow with joy and gratitude or with rancor and bitterness. The choice is ours.

When an adolescent refuses to be hugged or kissed, parents can resent the youth's attitude or redouble their silent love, their intercessory prayer, and affirm him or her in other areas of the youth's life. A partner may be indifferent to your love. You can react, retaliate, or withdraw; or you can use your imagination and ingenuity to discover and affirm some positive areas and interests in his or her life.

When Jesus was on the cross his nailed hands could not touch his mother or beloved disciple in fond farewell, but he could speak, "Woman, behold, your son! Behold, your mother!" It would have been useless to talk to his enemies; they would only have scoffed at him. But he could pray, "Father, forgive them; for they know not what they do." With what mobility Jesus redirected his caring, with what flexibility he rechanneled and continued the love flow.

# Dealing with Anger

If you are angry, do not let anger lead you into sin; do not let sunset find you still nursing it.

—*Ephesians 4:26 (NEB)*

"A good fight, like a thunderstorm, clears the atmosphere." But the lightning may have killed someone or set a house on fire. Fierce fighting between married couples can leave devastating psychological if not physical scars. Yet the fact is that people who deeply love each other can find themselves shouting in hatred or turning from each other in silent rage. What might have been love has changed its character and become hate. What to do?

The wise lover will seek at the earliest possible moment to recognize what is happening. He or she is convinced that unleashed rage destroys rather than builds, hurts not heals. Selfish outbursts of anger are counterproductive. They get results but they will call for ever greater outbursts to effect action the next time around, and thus the marriage plunges on a downward path. Furthermore, the action is induced by outward pressure on the partner rather than inspired by inner motivation.

I find, for my part, that I need to cultivate, first, the ability to recognize the approach of anger and then the desire to stop and deal with it then and there. For me this is the most difficult step. I need God's help. I flash some prayers to God. I am like an alcoholic; anger possesses me like a disease. I need to call on a Power greater than myself. Silent rage can grip me so that I do not think straight. I find myself recalling things from the past I had vowed to forget. Negative thoughts and venom flow through my veins. I withdraw into a haven of self-righteous spite. Others, with extroverted tendencies, will openly vent their anger on their partners, seeking release by hurting, seizing any verbal or even physical weapon to justify their position. Memory will harbor these wounds a long, long while. Tyrannizing a spouse through scolding, nagging, or ill-temper causes deep psychological wounds that jeopardize a marriage. If we are wise, we will turn to God for help before things have come to such a pass. We need that God who is a "present help in time of trouble." We need to see ourselves as powerless as alcoholics and humbly to ask for help. The issue we have been arguing about may or may not be justified, but the methods we have used have been unloving and wrong.

The moment a partner can say to God and the spouse, "I am angry, forgive me for letting my anger control me," that person is on the road toward reconciliation. Then can follow an opportunity for honest and loving dialogue.

Many couples have adopted the rule not to let the sun go down on their anger. There is untold value in establishing a habit of talking the day over at bedtime and clearing the decks before going to sleep. Honest encounter and apology, followed by forgiveness and reconciliation along with a prayer of thanksgiving to God, put the relationship back on track. More than that they deepen the love and cause it to grow even stronger and more exciting than it was before.

I recall a painful incident nearly fifty years ago during Holy Week. It was Good Friday, and I was to give one of the meditations on the Seven Last Words at a community church service. The participating ministers and their wives had been invited to enjoy a light lunch promptly at 11:30 since the service began at noon and the clergy were to process in with the choir. I was in the study at my church that morning and belatedly noticed the time. I phoned my wife that I would be right over to pick her up with our daughter for the luncheon and service.

I stopped at the house, honked the horn, waited one, two, three minutes, blowing the horn several times. Finally I went down the steps to the house and met her as she opened the door with our daughter ready to go to church. My first words were of blame and criticism that she had kept me waiting. She replied tartly that she had had trouble getting ready, and we rode to the church in grim silence. I was a divided self as I took part in that service: part of me self-righteously justifying my actions, part of me guiltily asking God for help as I was about to speak. I felt guilty and remorseful, and at the same time I was sure it was all her fault!

I was stubborn. All that Good Friday and all day Saturday I scarcely spoke to Irma. Inwardly I seethed; outwardly I sought to be controlled and put on a front before the children and the parishioners that I saw. I was outwardly pleasant but inwardly in turmoil. The first Good Friday, Jesus went the limit of love and self-giving. This Good Friday I was going the limit of stubbornness and self-love! Saturday, now as then, was a day of darkness. What an irony that I should be preparing an Easter sermon—a message of victory and joy—when I felt grim and defeated!

With the passing hours my turmoil increased. I went to bed Saturday night, but not a word passed between us. Finally I dropped off to sleep. About three o'clock I woke up, and the turmoil took on almost terror proportions as I thought of the upcoming two Easter services that day. Irma was sleeping beside me. By four o'clock I could stand it no longer, and I awakened her saying I had to talk with her. I asked her forgiveness for speaking so sharply and honking the horn so repeatedly. I told her of my inner turmoil and misery. Tears were in her eyes as well as mine as she asked me to forgive her for her icy attitude and frigid actions the last forty-eight hours. Our arms went around each other. There was healing and wholeness. Easter dawned with joy and celebration. Christ and love had indeed risen in our hearts that day.

These are steps that help to overcome anger:

1. Recognize your anger as soon as you can. As soon as possible admit it to yourself, to God, and to another (hopefully your spouse).

2. Seek the first opportunity to talk, write a note, or sit down with your partner. Be sure that you have sought to discover the hidden as well as apparent reasons for your anger: childhood behavior patterns, the desire to have your own way, to be "top dog." For my part I find that hidden reasons for my actions are still revealing themselves after all these years! I have often found that sitting in silence alone—or, better still, with my wife—gives opportunity for God to bring key thoughts to mind that unlock avenues to new ways of living.

3. Tell God and your mate of your share of the blame in the affair and ask their forgiveness.

If the last two steps are not sufficiently productive try detailed sharing with a trusted friend and/or putting your feelings on paper.

4. If you share with a trusted friend, choose someone who will keep your confidence, who is mature enough in faith and love not to be shocked or unsettled by your story, who will not sentimentally pity and excuse you, but who will love you enough to challenge you to aim for Jesus' standard of love, and who will pray with you and seal your new decision in the presence of God.

5. If you try putting pen to paper—journaling as it is called—these steps will prove helpful: unlock your deeper feelings and write out just what you feel. Get the negative ones out first and then reach down for the positive ones. Recall past shared experiences. Concentrate on your partner's needs and not the faults. Lay bare your *faults* rather than your *wants* and *desires.* Read and re-read what you have written. Add to it as you feel led. You will feel a new objectivity, a clarification of values, a desire to begin again.

One helpful method of journaling is to write a letter to God (Jesus). Write it in detail; write it for no other eyes than yours and God's. (It is your privilege to share it later if you so wish.) After re-reading it several times write a reply from God to you. Write down what you believe this all-knowing God of love wants to say to you. Finally—

6. Resolve not only to forgive, but to let bygones be bygones. Never drag up the past. Make a mental note of what gets you uptight: your spouse being late, too bossy, too messy, forgetting to relay

messages, or whatever, and resolve that you will be ready next time to take these things in stride. That partner of yours has so much on the plus side that you can well afford to overlook weaknesses and be grateful for the strengths.

CHAPTER ELEVEN

# Talking It Over

With acquaintances, you are forever aware of their slightly unreal image of you, and you edit yourself to fit. Many marriages are between acquaintances.

*John D. MacDonald*

The willingness to talk over a problem should be based on a genuine desire to find God's plan rather than the wife's or the husband's. It could be that the solution will end up being her way or his way, but it is much more likely to be a third way, God's way. The human desire frequently is for each to seek to have his or her way. On the other hand, in a burst of unselfish love, one may say, "Let's do it your way," just to be nice or to make up for some past act of selfishness. Either of these methods avoid the challenge of seeking to find out God's will.

Vacation time was approaching. I wanted to go to the mountains; my wife wanted to be near a lake. Each of us in our individual ways wanted to get away from people and responsibility. I had avoided talking it over with Irma, fearing that I would feel that I should have to be unselfish and give up my plan to go to the mountains.

Finally we took time to talk and discovered that we had both of us been suppressing the thought that Agnes, a single woman and close friend of ours, would like to be invited to share in our vacation plans. As we talked, it broke in on both of us that this was clearly God's plan. Agnes readily accepted our invitation. We had a beautiful month in a rented cottage on a lake, teaching our youngsters to swim, bringing untold joy to Agnes, and returning home rested and invigorated.

Discovering and obeying God's plan often introduces a new dimension into a marriage. If a couple is willing to be silent in each other's presence, each asking, "God, what is your plan for me?" thoughts are turned from self toward God and his plan for us. "When man listens, God speaks." He brings to mind buried, unfinished business as well as unthought of serendipities.

Listening to God can be painful, but more often it is sheer joy. Buried hurts will surface. Now these can be dealt with. Sometimes I discover hidden selfish motives at work. Childhood patterns reappear. More often thoughts and ideas leap to mind that are timely and strategic. What fun it is!

TV, children, church, and community activities, to say nothing of the pressures of work, conspire to rob us of time together. But this together time is imperative. It is a must. Sometimes it will happen that both will just be together and in a mood for talking. But whatever the circumstance let us give high priority to finding time for this type of communication. Be willing to turn off the TV, to ask the kids to wait, even on occasion to give up going to a meeting or social event in order to find time for a heart-to-heart talk.

The verbal person needs to hold back, sharing deeply but sparingly, never advising or prodding. Be patient and wait until the quiet one talks a little, and then receive the communication with tender caring as one would treasure a beautiful gift. Let neither try to control or guide the conversation. Let each be willing to expose and give of himself or herself regardless of cost or fear of rejection and to leave the results with God and the working of his Spirit.

Try to be sensitive to the first approaches of negative moods, tensions, fears, hurts, anger. Do not, in self-sufficiency, think you can handle them alone. Share your need at the moment. How often I have phoned home from the church study, or long distance when traveling, to share a need with Irma and to have a prayer over the phone. It does not take long. The humility and willingness to do it is the key to power.

When you talk together, move quickly to the feeling level. Be willing to express feelings of hurt, of loneliness, of uselessness and purposelessness, of unfulfilled dreams, of joy and gratitude, of hopes fulfilled, of the excitement or the boredom of tomorrow. Let the partner listen without seeking to advise, scold, or change the other. We all have a right to our own feelings. Often when one tells of moods of inadequacy or inferiority the other will share similar feelings. It is exciting to discover the hunger for a deeper love in each other's hearts. One day when Irma and I were talking, I said to her, "I feel so inadequate to love you the way I want to and the way you deserve." How close I felt to her when she expressed similar feelings and longings.

Happiness is two people discovering that each is lonely. Friendship is two people receiving and accepting each other's loneliness.

CHAPTER TWELVE

# The Will to Love

A husband said that it was as if there was a brick wall between him and his wife. I asked him if he were to find a gate through that brick wall, would he go through it? His emphatic *no* helped him to understand that the barrier between him and his wife was inside himself rather than outside.

*—Dr. Paul Welter*

Love is patient and kind; love is not jealous or boastful; it is not arrogant or rude. Love does not insist on its own way; it is not irritable or resentful; it does not rejoice at wrong, but rejoices in the right. Love bears all things, believes all things, hopes all things, endures all things.

*—I Corinthians 13:4-7*

During the last decade I have tried to keep abreast of at least some of the literature on relational living, behavioral tendencies, and counseling techniques. I am sure that my skills have improved and that I have gained some competence in this field. But as this ability to analyze and evaluate people grew I was surprised to discover an adverse side effect. I found myself looking at members of my own family with the eyes of a critic!

If my wife gave me advice, she was trying to control me; if she failed to give advice, she was not sufficiently concerned with my interests. If she talked too freely in public she was upstaging me; if she failed to carry the conversation along, she was not using the talents God gave her. No matter what she did I was in the critic's corner. Slowly I was being consumed by a desire to analyze and to sit in judgment. No matter what she did she couldn't win! I was the winner: evaluating and pigeon-holing. But what I lost was infinitely more important, for I discovered that as this critical attitude entered one door my love was going out of the other.

In addition to this, my wife's health, long a hindrance to her public speaking, improved so much during these years that she was now able to travel with me and share the speaking during my engagements. After the sessions one or two persons would approach me, but ten or fifteen would surround her! I was jealous! This jealousy was added to my critical attitude, and I felt the reservoirs of love running low.

It was at this point I saw that the needed change must take place within me, rather than in her. I had been looking at the speck in her eye, entirely oblivious to the beam in my own! I longed for more love toward her to offset jealousy and critical attitudes. But the verb *love* has no imperative mood. We cannot command ourselves to love. Love is a gift of God, often taking us by surprise. A man in the throes of critical attitudes and jealousy cannot say, "I'm going to love." Love bubbles; it flows as does water from an artesian well.

As I prayed about my jealousy, the thought flashed over me, "Start thanking God for the way he is using her." This I could do and did. At first I acted mechanically. It felt awkward to put this gratitude into words. But as I persisted, thanksgiving began joyously and gratefully to well up from a full heart. Unbidden and yet so welcome, love began to stream into my heart, and the jealousy was gone. Whenever it returned, I had only to repeat the procedure, and the miracle always happened.

My critical attitudes came in for a longer treatment. I saw that by analyzing my wife I depersonalized her and she was no longer the lovely woman of whom I was so fond. When the botanist examines a flower, pulling off leaves and petals and spreading it all out, he no longer has a flower. A choice must be made—the parts or the whole! Likewise I had to choose between being critically aware of what Irma did or rejoicing in the woman she was and thanking God for whatever she did. As I stopped analyzing and started giving thanks again the deeper miracle happened. Love flooded my heart.

Now there is a postscript to this story: day by day growth and changes in Irma also took place. But let me underscore this statement *that change in her was farthest from my thoughts.* I was the one who needed to change. I was the one to whom God was speaking. Had I done any of the above with a hidden motive to change Irma it would have backfired. God would not have been in it. My love would have been hypocritical and therefore powerless. As it was, God used my willingness to cease being critical and jealous, my willingness to practice thanksgiving and affirmation as powerful change agents in both of our lives.

Critical attitudes such as we have described are negative and love destroying. The positive counterpart is to develop skills in discernment. Here we become aware of and evaluate our partner's actions, motives, or feelings, not with a desire to criticize or correct, but in order to discover places of need where we can be supportive, places of loneliness where we can share love. It is the loneliness, the hurt, the need in life that foster the desire for aggressiveness (or withdrawal), rebellion, antagonism. If we minister with genuine love to these primeval hungers we make possible change in our partners and maturation in ourselves.

At the heart of every marriage is a decision relative to the will to love. Often the love is conditional: "I'll love you if you love me," "I'll fulfill my role as wife if you fulfill yours as a husband." Our love then becomes dependent on the behavior of our partner. We lean on each other. Whereas in an unconditional marriage each partner leans on God and draws unlimited supplies of love from him. We are not ultimately conditioned by our spouse's behavior.

It may upset us for a while if we discover that our mate is not growing and maturing as we believe he or she should, or is slipping into one of the addictions, or is unfaithful, or quits church, or refuses to associate with our friends. But our commitment to love is a willingness to go one hundred percent of the way regardless of what our partner does. It is a one hundred to zero proposition. God's love as modeled for us by Jesus is this one hundred to nothing brand. Regardless of what we do, God goes one hundred percent of the way, all the time, loving us in every situation. With his help we can try to do the same.

Love is not, then, primarily a matter of the emotions. It is a commitment of the will. God wills to love us, come what may. His covenant through the ages has been, "I will be your God and you shall be my people." To fall in love under God is to share this quality of commitment with one's partner. This kind of a pact unlocks doors to exciting shared experiences, to new adventures in love and joys beyond description. The road is costly and difficult, but, as we travel it, problems are transcended and the marriage is continually being cemented with an ever-deepening love.

But what if only one of the couple will accept this life-style? Must the other one go it alone? Jesus did! Still living his hundred to nothing style of life, going all the way all the time! It is lonely; it is hard, but still it is exciting and rewarding.

I recall scores of partners—sometimes the man, sometimes the woman—in my seventy years in the ministry, living this hundred to nothing life-style while married to partners who dragged their feet. When I first met Joan she had her arm in a sling. Her alcoholic husband had beaten her up again. This had been the story of this marriage for fifteen years. "Should I get a divorce?" she asked me.

The religious cleric inside of me wanted to say, "No, of course, you shouldn't get a divorce," but I knew she could say, "You've never been beaten up by a drunken husband. You've never stayed awake night after night in terror, dreading the sound of his footstep." The male within me wanted to reach out in chivalry. I wanted to take her in my arms, comfort her, and protect her from such a brute of a husband. In no way could I possibly urge her to go back to him.

We talked together of the great love of God as seen in Jesus on the cross: reviled, spat on, nailed, killed. I asked her to sit in the little chapel adjacent to my study, and ask God what she should do. In twenty minutes she came back. I was amazed to see the smile amid the tears and to hear the assurance in her

voice. "I'm going back to *love* him," she said. "I've been cleaning up his vomit in bitterness. I've been undressing him with loathing. I'm going back to do these things in love and for Christ's sake." I felt greatly humbled by the degree of this woman's commitment. How unworthy I was to be her pastor!

Yes, there were more beatings, another broken bone; but three and a half years later Joan's husband responded to the love of God mediated through her, and the miracle happened. He responded to Joan's request to attend Alcoholics Anonymous meetings. He called on and accepted the Power greater than himself. He became a changed man. "Yes," said Joan, "it was worth it. I'd do it all again. How much I've learned! How good God has been!"

CHAPTER THIRTEEN

# Celebrating Love

How do I love thee? Let me count the ways.
I love thee to the depth and breadth and height
My soul can reach, when feeling out of sight
For the ends of being and ideal grace.
I love thee to the level of every day's
Most quiet need, by sun and candlelight.
I love thee freely as men strive for the right.
I love thee purely, as they turn from praise.
I love thee with the passion put to use
In my old griefs, and with my childhood's faith.
I love thee with a love I seemed to lose
With my lost saints. I love thee with the breath,
Smiles, tears of all my life; and, if God choose,
I shall but love thee better after death.

*—Elizabeth Barrett Browning*

The secular spouse *makes* love, the God-fearing spouse *celebrates* love. The man who operates without God feels himself to be in charge of his life and so as a self-made man he aims to *make* good, *make* a success, *make* love. The children of God know that life and love are gifts of God. They do not make or author them, but as they live in obedience to God, the heavenly Father out of his treasures gives these gifts his children can enjoy and celebrate. True celebration is not external activity calculated to induce happiness and escape boredom. It is a recognition of and response to the joys of the spirit that God has already given us.

Frank is an insurance salesman. He has irregular hours. His time of coming home to meals had been a sore point with his wife, Peg. Of late he has been pretty good about phoning when he realized he would be late. Peg feels a little easier in her mind now about his being on time; so this night she put on two steaks, planning an especially nice dinner. It is one of their special days—the anniversary of the day they met at that church social. "Frank won't think of it," she muses, "but perhaps he'll remember when he sees the candlelight and steaks."

Frank is late again! He gets to talking with a prospect in the city and finally arrives nearly an hour late. Peg is debating whether to explode or to wait for his apology. But his apology is slow in coming, and so she explodes, "Your dinner is spoiled!" She does not say "our dinner," but "your dinner." There is a barb in her words. He defends himself with, "You can't expect an insurance man always to be on time to meals." Nothing more is said at the moment. They have long since learned not to make a big deal out of every incident. But as they sit down to eat, they know they are not in fellowship. They are so near, yet miles apart.

Frank tries to hide the sense of separation by recounting a humorous incident that occurred that afternoon. But he feels phony. The conversation settles down to exciting sentences like, "Please pass the salt"; "I think I'll have another slice of bread." The impasse could be broken in a moment if either one were willing to say, "I am sorry." Peg is thinking: "He might at least apologize. He was the one who was late." Frank is thinking, "She snapped at me without giving me time to explain."

If Frank would only say: "Peg, forgive me. I'm still the same stinker you met thirty years ago. Sorry I was late again." Then in a minute hands could have gone across the table, or they might have risen and met half way with a kiss and embrace. They deeply love each other, but each is tired and stubborn. Neither one has the courage or humility to apologize, and the meal drags on.

Soon Peg goes out to do the dishes, and Frank seeks to rid himself of his uncomfortable feelings by going out into the kitchen, taking a towel, and starting to dry the dishes. He is trying to work his way back. He is seeking by a physical act to make up for a spiritual deficiency. Or later that night he comes back from a call bringing Peg a box of candy.

Once more he is seeking to pay for the sins of his soul by the fruits of his body. His loving act has an ulterior motive to it, and whenever love has "an angle" it is suspect.

God does not love us with any ulterior motive of making amends or making us "good." He loves us because we are his children, because he is crazy about us. Speaking of standing by his children; God says, "I . . . for mine own sake, I do it" (Isaiah 37:35; 48:11).

God's caring is the overflow of sterling love. Frank's love is geared to results. He is trying to make good will where there is none. Later that night he says to Peg in the vernacular of the secular man, "Let's go to bed and make love." He is hoping that two bodies coming together will draw two hearts along with them. He longs for a warm response, which will be very slow in coming, for no real healing of the hurt has taken place.

Now let us suppose that our story takes a different turn at the table. One of the two has the courage and humility to break through the impasse. Let us suppose it is Frank. He gets up, walks around the table, and says: "Peg, I'm sorry I forgot to phone. I might at least have done that much when I saw how late I would be." Immediately there will be a response. Within seconds Peg has spoken of her sharp words, and love has flowed again and is celebrated with a kiss and embrace. They are knit together.

Now Frank goes out in the kitchen to wipe the

dishes—not to work his way back, but to *celebrate the fact that he is back*. The box of candy is given that evening not *in order that* they may be close in heart, but *because* they are close. It is to celebrate their oneness of spirit. He is not trying to create or make good will between them. Their obedience to God (confession and repentance) had enabled them to receive the love that he was offering to them. When later that evening Frank said, "Let's go to bed and love each other," it was not two bodies dragging two unwilling hearts, but two eager hearts already joined in love drawing together two bodies with fervor and rejoicing. They were not "making" love. They were "celebrating" the love that God had already given them.

The mood of celebration is a fragile thing. A word of fault-finding or the taking of a partner for granted can destroy it in a moment. A wife at one of our retreats said, "I am much more ready to love my husband in bed if he loves me in the living room." She knew what it was to be treated as an "it" throughout the day and then to be called on to be a warm, self-giving lover at night. All of us resent being treated as impersonal conveniences and then, when the partner's mood changes, being suddenly called on to switch roles and become a loving, caring spouse.

The wise lover cultivates an early awareness of moods and feelings that divide partners. Ready acknowledgment of one's inner needs and quick apology are sure steps to bridge any separation. Love starts to flow again in response to need and apology, and the mood for celebration returns. This mood finds expression in countless ways: a knowing smile, a meal together at a favorite eating place, a trip to a trysting place full of memories, a quiet evening at home, a shopping spree, kneeling beside each other at Communion, arms locked around each other in love.

CHAPTER FOURTEEN

# Listening Is Loving

I sat where they sat.

—*Ezekiel 3:15 (KJV)*

Recently, at a conference, a young and successful businessman sought me out to talk about his relationship with his wife. They had had an unusually happy courtship. The first years of marriage had gone well in spite of some growing pains in their relating to each other. But now she was pregnant. She was no longer the same carefree girl of the dating days. Her words were sharp and harsh, her temper short, her disposition bitchy. How could he relate to her?

During the first years of marriage he had been spending more and more time in his business. He had been successful; he was making good money. His wife had grown lonely during those evenings he was at the office, but had managed to accept these lonesome hours as part of the price of his success. But now, her disposition had changed. She no longer accepted but resented her evenings alone. She snapped at him when he came in late at night. He, on the other hand, had been spending more and more time away from home. To be away from home was to be away from trouble.

We spoke together of the causes for his wife's discomfort and apprehension, the fact that she was not really herself. "Yes," he replied; "she is like a stranger to me!" We talked of her need of love. These were days when cherishing and tenderness were doubly necessary for her. I could almost see the thoughts take shape in his mind as he was slowly determining to be more tender, to take away more time from his business, to be home evenings, and to minister to this woman who needed him. But, somehow, one knew it would all be a matter of kindness, almost of duty, rather than springing from joyous love.

It was then that God gave me the thought to say to him: "Bill, this woman is not only a stranger to you, she is a stranger to herself. She does not understand what is going on inside of her. She is shocked to find herself scolding you and screaming at you. She is torn apart, wanting to be that person that you loved so much when you were dating her. Instead she finds herself acting like an old witch and hating herself for it. She cannot understand what is going on inside of her."

Immediately I felt a shift in his position; a change of stance. No longer was he thinking of overlooking her faults, nor of his difficulty in relating to her. Now his whole being was transferred into the very center of her life. He was truly listening to her. He was seeing and loving her from within herself.

This is the genius of the Incarnation. God did not only look at us from his point of view, but came down in the human flesh of Jesus so that he could express his love from within us. This becomes even more true as God dwells in us through his Holy Spirit and loves us from within, sharing in our needs and insecurities. He guides us from within so that he is not a God from without trying to relate to us because he is so good and wonderful, but rather a God who has moved over onto our side and who has taken up residence within us. It is from this stance (locus) that he loves and affirms us. So this young man saw his wife as if from within herself. His heart, deeply touched, became wide open with tender love and caring. In just a few days their home was made new.

It is one thing to reach out from a place of security with an abundance of kindness and goodwill. Then one feels sorry for people and wants to help them. But it is another thing to seek to move over into the center of another's being so that our insight and love spring up from where they are rather than from where we are.

Listening is an effective way of loving. A spouse speaks to the partner and the reply is, "Yes, go ahead. I'm listening." But he goes on reading the newspaper, or she continues to write that letter. If I can lay aside what I am doing and listen to my wife—perhaps a tale of trouble, perhaps a happy little surprise to share—she feels important and loved. Listening is a wonderful way of caring.

A good listener hears not only the words that are spoken, but unspoken words of hidden and suppressed emotions. I came home eight hours late from a Midwestern trip. It was bad weather. Plane flights were delayed and canceled. I had managed to phone that I would be at least four hours late, but I could not get to a phone after that. When I finally arrived at home eight hours late, Irma met me with sharp words, reproving me for being late and worrying her so. "You must never go away again like this," she said. I, of course, was weary and so eager for the warmth and security of my own home. I am sure that forty years before this I would have answered sharply, "*You*'re worried! What about *me*?" or something in that vein. But now, as soon as she spoke, I knew she had been concerned for my safety and had worried lest an accident might have happened. What she was really saying was: "Lee, I've missed you so much. I couldn't bear it if something happened to you. I'm so glad you are safely home." What a fool I would have been to retort to her spoken words, when they covered such fears and longings. So I just walked over to her, put my arms around her, and said: "Yes, Honey, and I missed you, too. Isn't it good to be together again." There were tears of joy in my eyes as well as in hers.

To listen is to be able to act from the other's situation rather than our own. Then a man, even though tired at the end of the day, will offer not scolding or advice but strong arms and warm words of love to the frantic mother. The wife, weary herself, will offer her flesh to the discouraged or fatigued husband that they may celebrate together.

Tom's father had died. He and Sue were returning home from the funeral. Tom had been responsible for family plans and, with Sue, for meeting the guests. The three-hundred-mile drive left them both exhausted. All Sue thought of was bed and sleep. But she discovered that Tom had been thinking of bed and sex. It seemed strange to her that Tom would come from his father's funeral and turn to her for sexual fulfillment. It was weeks later when it came to her that his father's death was to Tom as though he had lost part of himself. He was now only part of a man. But as he poured the strength of his manhood into her body, he felt fulfilled and made whole again. Yes, she reflected, it was like resurrection after death. Yes, she would offer herself again and again to this man who again and again was so patient and tender toward her.

CHAPTER FIFTEEN

# Shared Experiences

Sharing is the whole meaning of my life. Nothing in this life exists for me at all until and unless I can share it. This is true of everything in my life. There is no sunset however beautiful, no joke however funny, no poem, no voyage, no movie, no meal even that I can enjoy only by myself.

*—Leonard Bernstein*

One of the joys of marriage is the increasing number of *firsts* experienced together. Memory recollects (re-collects) them: the first look, the first touch, the first kiss, the first vocal "I love you." Engagement, marriage, and honeymoon add their joyous memories. There are the firsts of sexuality, the discovery of pregnancy, the first signs of life, the birth itself, now so frequently including the husband in the delivery room. The first Christmas is beautiful, but the first Christmas with a two- or three-year-old child is still more wonderful. So the firsts multiply. Realism demands that we include the first quarrel and also the first sorrow. They are part of life's rosary: "Memories that bless and burn."

Irma and I had been married about three years. I have forgotten what came up between us. I was probably stubborn, or Irma might have spoken sharply. But we both remember that evening now over sixty years ago. Irma lay on the bed in a room off the living room. I was in my study, also off the living room. I heard her crying, but I would not go in to her. As she stopped crying she heard me in the rocking chair as the floor boards creaked, but she would not leave the bed. Twenty, thirty minutes passed. Then Irma came out and walked into my study. Her eyes were red from crying. She sat on the floor at my feet and laid her head on my knee and said: "Lee, the days fly too fast for us to waste them like this. Let's pray together and begin again." Something in me melted, and I put my arms around her and we walked into the bedroom together and knelt there asking God to forgive us. He not only forgave us but flooded us with his love. We were knit together more closely than ever.



Perhaps God in his wisdom was preparing us

better to meet the death of our second son, Charles. He was a healthy baby, the heaviest and tallest at birth of any of our children. At seven months he came down with meningitis and died within forty-eight hours. There was the disbelief; it could not be that our healthy, growing little fellow had died. Acceptance and thanksgiving began to follow. God had loaned this beautiful boy to us for seven months. How we had loved him!

Charles' going proved to be a blessed, if poignant experience. We had been stern disciplinarians to our older son. Charles' loss softened us, made Lionel much more precious to us. Irma and I found that we needed each other at a deeper level than ever before. Our love grew and mellowed. Death had opened the doors to life. We were learning to discover that all of life can be beautiful under God. "In everything God works for good with those who love him" (Romans 8:28).

There are the adjustment experiences. Often the partners in a marriage have come from different cultural and/or ethnic backgrounds. They have been brought up in different family traditions. How shall they celebrate Christmas? One family has thrown the tinsel on the tree, helter-skelter; the other stretched each piece carefully over the branches. One tradition opened presents first, the other after an orderly breakfast. There are customs and traditions that have been handed down through the generations. These differences can occasion tension or even a quarrel. Each couple must establish its own patterns, including now this now that from the past, but basically creating new traditions that are their very own.

There are the happy serendipities: summer vacations, picnics, family pets, camping, climbing, canoeing, swimming, golfing; evenings with music, books, or TV.

There are the tasks we undertake together. Many couples teach a church-school class together or lead a youth group. Many find an inner-city or community project. Irma and I have stood shoulder to shoulder for fifty years in the pastorate. Seven or eight of the last fifteen years we have traveled together through this country and Canada as co-leaders in retreats and renewal missions. We have given our witness at meeting after meeting. The response has invariably been that, though the content of our messages was helpful, the most moving factor was that we stood there together opening our hearts about our relationship to each other and to God. Our togetherness in itself has been a powerful witness.

Partners in marriage reveal from time to time uneven strengths and weaknesses. Frequently when I am depressed, Irma proves to be a tower of strength. When she is in need, I respond with love and affirmation. I recall when I was having a nervous breakdown fifty or so years ago. I spent three months in a sanitarium. Irma, three months pregnant, kept the home fires burning, mothered our children, remained buoyant and smiling through my depressions. Her visits to me brought hope. She believed in me and that I would come through and be better than ever. She was as an anchor in the storm. Such an experience deepens and cements love and makes the marriage tie more precious than ever. The total recovery took nine months. What a brick she was! How much of what I am today I owe to her!

The converse is also true. Let me quote verbatim the story Irma recently told at one of our retreats: "I was overcome by a deep depression. I suddenly realized how alone I was. My parents were gone, my brother and sister both dead. I was the last of my line. I felt like a motherless child. Contrary to my usually buoyant self, I felt life not worth living. I called out to my husband, 'Lee, I feel so lonely.' Immediately he left his study and came to me. 'Lonely, with me here?' he said. He bent over and kissed me. He held out his arms. I stood up and he held me close. The loneliness disappeared. Life was OK again."

It is fun to do some things together, and fun to do some things alone. There's a place for sharing and a place for solitude. A friend of mine likes to garden with his wife, but to go fishing alone. My wife did not share the mountain trips with me and the children; she stayed at home and read. But we enjoyed eating out and going to the theater and symphony together.

What holds potential for good also holds potential for evil. The emotion and commitment that go to build shared experiences can move in the opposite direction making for bitter competition. Partners can undermine each other, belittling and diminishing each other. There can be a constant power play to gain the upper hand. The competition can include the children as one partner plays the children against the other. Rewards of money by the father, special love and petting by the mother can be pitted against each other. Any couples that live in this way can take heart, knowing that God can change the direction of these negative attitudes and, with their willingness, direct them toward the rich sharing we have been describing.

Building togetherness can be fun, filling life with happy memories. Everything can draw you closer together when it is a shared experience with love as an ingredient. The experiences run the gamut from waiting for a baby's arrival to sitting in the doctor's office while he tells you that your partner has cancer. They can be financial as together a couple works to pull out of debt or establish a business. It is the togetherness that counts, the standing side by side, supporting, trusting, believing in each other.

When God is there with his love, you stand hand in hand, laughing together, weeping together. It is all in the bundle of life. When Irma and I stood beside the grave of our little child, we had God and each other; we had another little child and the future.

Togetherness often is costly—one or the other giving up original plans, trusting the partner's ideas, going along with the other's wishes. Surprises can be fun. On our eighth wedding anniversary I packed a lunch, put picnic paraphernalia in the car and said: "Honey, dress for a picnic. We're going out, no questions asked." It was a great day as we picnicked at a scenic spot near the foot of Chittenango Falls in central New York. We still talk of it.

# God Is in Your Marriage

Surely the Lord is in this place; and I did not know it.

—*Genesis 28:16*

Back in your dating days, do you remember saying, "It seems as if we've always known each other," or, "Our love will last forever"? *Always* and *forever* are God language. Did you ever say, "It seems as though we were meant for each other"? Who meant you for each other? Even though you may not have realized it, even though you may not have named his name, God was already in your courtship, affirming your falling in love. He was saying "Yes, I am in this dream of yours calling you to be each other's forever. I am giving you my love, which is a never-ending, eternal love. No wonder you feel as though you belong to each other forever. It is my joy to draw you together with bonds of love. Seek my will and your marriage will live forever." God honors our faith in each other and our decision to build a home together. He floods our lives with his love and blesses our marriage with his presence.

Some of us, however, may have married for quite different reasons. It may have been a shotgun wedding, a marriage of convenience, or a hasty marriage entered into on the rebound. You may have divorced one mate and married another, even taken him or her from another partner. None of this means that God is through with you. There will be heartache and pain. There will be guilt to be confessed, processed, and forgiven. Nevertheless, God forgives; God enters into your present marriage and makes you and your spouse his choice for each other under the present circumstances. He had another original plan in mind for you. But since you and/or your spouse blew it, he has offered you another opportunity. This can be exciting and wonderful beyond measure, although it will be a difficult and costly road for you will face the temptations that trapped you before.

Jim, the father of a twelve-year-old boy, told me this story. "I was dating Laura, and to me she was just another girl. She became pregnant. We were not engaged or even contemplating marriage. The months dragged on, and we had to make a decision.

We decided to give the child a home where there would be both a father and a mother, so we got married—not for love, but to give the kid a home. Over twelve years have gone by and we've stuck to our agreement, but there is no love in our home. How can there be?"

When Jim and Laura decided to do what they believed to be the right thing, I told him—to marry to give the boy a home—at that moment God entered into their marriage, offering them a fresh gift of his love. He told this to his wife. Tears came to their eyes, the guilt of the years melted away, and they embraced each other in genuine newfound love. From then on their life was lived on a different plane.

Let us be assured of God's presence in our marriages whether we have felt God's blessings from the very beginnings of courtship or have turned to God after months or years of disobedience to his will. God is eager to break into our marriages and enable us to grow and mature in his love. His ultimate plan is that each of our homes will become a miniature of his heavenly kingdom.

God is love. He has made us in his image. Therefore the deepest and most real part of ourselves is our potential and capacity for love. We are inherently created for relating, for loving, for warm interaction. Persons are fulfilling the basic drive of their being when they love. For a man and woman to fall into and grow in love together is of the very essence of God.

God is love, and love is God. I remember some sixty-eight years ago when Irma and I were falling in love, we stood on a north Wisconsin hillside looking into the golden west. The sky was like a molten furnace. Fiery yellows and reds leaped across the heavens. We stood in mute wonder, and later broke into song together:

> Day is dying in the west;
> Heaven is touching earth with rest;
> Wait and worship while the night
> Sets her evening lamps alight
> Through all the sky.
> Holy, holy, holy, Lord God of Hosts!
> Heaven and earth are full of thee!
> Heaven and earth are praising thee,
> O Lord most high!

Our arms had drawn more tightly around each other, and together we felt the presence of God. It was a triangular thrust of God breaking in on us. We were growing closer to each other and to him. If we had not spoken or sung his name, God would still have been there. But to affirm his love and to name his name made his presence come more alive within us.

Many couples remember the time and place where they first said out loud to each other those magic words: "I love you." Previously thoughts had come to mind: "I love him or her. I wonder if he or she loves me. Won't he ever ask me? Will she say yes if I do ask her?" Even thinking these thoughts deepens love. But the very act of saying them out loud causes the love to move forward by leaps and bounds. Fortunate is that couple whose love, day by day, is enthusiastically put into words.

The presence of God in marriage gives long-term commitment. When God made the covenant with Abraham, he unconditionally committed himself to be the God of Israel, come what may and without limit. "I will be your God," he said to Moses, "and you shall be my people" (Leviticus 26:12). He used the analogy of marriage to describe his relation to his people; "I will betroth you to me for ever . . . in steadfast love, and in mercy" (Hosea 2:19).

Today's culture tends to emphasize short-term commitments. It is the age of the fast buck, quick sex, the shot in the arm, the pep pill, the lottery ticket, sudden winnings, and excitements. "I want mine fast and I want it now." These modern trends so infiltrate our thinking and inner being that we too are tempted to make short-term and temporary commitments with each other. But this God of ours who has brought us together in couples is the God of "the everlasting covenant," the God of long-term and eternal commitments. Our love, rooted in God, is a growing, never-ending love. Our commitment is "as long as we both shall live." Life and love forever!

Giving thanks at mealtimes, taking out time for morning and/or evening prayers is not just a pious practice. Genuine prayer keeps us in touch with the God who is the source of love. It cultivates in us openness and humility that enables us to keep our marriage authentic.

The world boasts an "eternal triangle" where a third party threatens and often destroys a marriage. This kind of triangle belies its name. God's presence, however, in our marriage forms a triangle that is truly eternal. Eagerly he supplies us with newness of love day by day. With the constancy of ocean tides his love flows and overflows in our lives. The joy of God is a marriage fully alive and aglow with his love.

# EPILOGUE

*(An Afterword That Is Really a Foreword)*

## THE MARRIAGE SERVICE

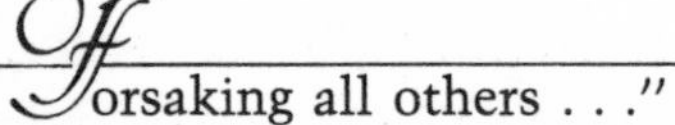

"Forsaking all others . . ."

"To have and to hold, from this day forward, for better or worse, for richer or poorer, in sickness and in health, to love and to cherish 'til death us do part."

You have heard the reasons for living together without marriage: "If we've promised to love each other, what difference does it make to tell it in front of a minister? . . . A wedding certificate is just a piece of paper. . . . We save hundreds of dollars a year in taxes by not marrying. . . . It's our business and this is the way we like it. . . . If we change our minds we don't have to mess around with any divorce." And so on.

But deep in our hearts are urgings that draw us toward marriage. We feel bonded to man and to God, to society and to all that is eternal.

A couple does not live to themselves. They are members of society. When a catastrophe or tragedy comes we need and depend on neighbors. When sickness comes—a child may be born handicapped—we turn to the medical community. We find that we need doctors, nurses, hospitals, and institutions made possible by a generous community. Unemployment or health insurance payments, and later on Social Security checks, remind us that today we do not live alone or to ourselves. The day comes quickly when we welcome the support of the community in which we live. To ridicule or to shrug off the time-tested customs of society is to undermine the communal strengths that we will be needing some day. To elope or live together without ceremony can often be a desire for freedom from the pressures of family and friends. Our lives are impoverished and hemmed in when we shut out those who love us and have contributed to our growth and development. Society and history have amply demonstrated that on the stability of the home rests the strength of a community and nation.

Of greater significance is the joy of retelling the love story before God and friends. To fall in love is to experience something of eternity. God has entered into the mortal lives of two human beings. It is an echo of the incarnation—God who is love, coming again into human flesh and drawing together two people who were once completely unknown to each other.

Let us go through the wedding ceremony and see it as a recapitulation of a couple's love story. The wedding service offers the opportunity to dramatize this event as we celebrate its telling in the presence of God and friends.

The tradition of groom and bride not seeing each other on the wedding day serves to recall the time when the couple had not yet met each other. They come to church separately and enter by different doors, thus dramatizing the time when they were growing up unknown to each other. Their coming to the church is indicative of a God who has called them to each other and is uniting them in his love.

The couple enters the sanctuary by concerted plan from different doors escorted by members of their respective families or their personal friends. The separateness of the families is further emphasized by the seating arrangement. The bride usually enters on her father's arm, and the groom is eager for that first look recalling the "enchanted evening when across a crowded room" he "saw and knew." Each step down the aisle symbolizes the deepening friendship, ripening into love through the months, possibly years. Their primary loyalties are still to their respective families, but they dream dreams of togetherness. They feel God's call to be husband and wife.

The opening part of the wedding service with its declaration of purpose and promise "to forsake all others" focuses attention on the time when they slowly transferred their primary loyalty from their families and other friends to each other. This is dramatically portrayed as the parents "give away" the bride. The groom's parents may also "give away" the groom. Each set of parents may light the two candles on the altar for their respective children. The children, now bride and groom, later take their candles to light the center candle representing their marriage. The couple are now joined hand in hand before the congregation joyously proclaiming the love that united them months before at their engagement. In their hearts they pledged and repledged their vows during the days and weeks that followed the engagement. Now they declare these vows that all may know and celebrate with them.

The movement forward toward the altar dramatizes the increasing closeness that the couple has felt through the months both toward each other and toward God. The minister symbolizes the presence of the heavenly Father who is now affirming the love he has given these young people. God promises to surround them with his protective care, to lead them on in this new and exciting land of love with its home building and opportunities of service.

The exchange of rings and the sacrament of the Lord's Supper, which is often received at this time, give tangible evidence that two people now belong to each other and to God. It is a dual pledge: to God who is the unending source of the love that will hold them together and to each other in times of plenty and want, in fair weather and foul.

The service closes with the couple walking down the aisle and leaving arm in arm by the same door. They are united as they go out into the world, little knowing what lies ahead. But that can wait. They have told their story. To them, the minister did not marry them. It was God who started it all by causing them to fall in love. The minister symbolized this God and enabled them to "tell the world" of God's calling them together and of their love for each other.

Each has discovered someone with whom to share the adventure of living. They have declared this before their friends and their God. This love is for keeps. It is forever!